DATE DUE

FEB 2 1 2006	
MAR 1 0 2008	
MAY 1 8 2009	

BRODART, CO.　　　　　　　Cat. No. 23-221-003

Thomas Paine

Heroes of the American Revolution

★

Don McLeese

Rourke
Publishing LLC
Vero Beach, Florida 32964

www.rourkepublishing.com

PHOTO CREDITS: Cover Portrait, Title page, Pages 11, 13, 19, 28, 29 from the Library of Congress; Pages 9, 20, 23, 27 ©North Wind Picture Archives; CoverScene, Pages 5, 14, 24, ©Getty Images; Pages 6, 10 ©Poppyland Photos Page 16 from the U.S. National Guard

Title page: *An illustration of Thomas Paine*

Editor: Frank Sloan

Cover and page design by Nicola Stratford

Library of Congress Cataloging-in-Publication Data

McLeese, Don.
   Thomas Paine / Don McLeese.
      p. cm. -- (Heroes of the American Revolution)
   Includes bibliographical references and index.
   ISBN 1-59515-215-6
 1. Paine, Thomas, 1737-1809--Juvenile literature. 2. Political scientists--United States--Biography--Juvenile literature. 3. Revolutionaries--United States--Biography--Juvenile literature. 4. United States--History--Revolution, 1775-1783--Juvenile literature. I. Title. II. Series: McLeese, Don. Heroes of the American Revolution.
 JC178.V5M38 2004
 320.51'092--dc22

                              2004007604

Printed in the USA

LB/LB

Table of Contents

---★---

The Right to be Free

★

Thomas Paine was a great thinker and a great writer. Some people even said he was a **genius**. Thomas was a hero of the American Revolution because his writing convinced people who lived in America that the United States should become its own country. Instead of being ruled by England, the people who lived in America should rule themselves.

Thomas wrote this in a short **pamphlet** that he named *Common Sense*. As the title says, *Common Sense* was something that the common man and woman could understand. It would make sense to them. He said that America should declare its **independence** from England.

Before long, America did just that! It issued the Declaration of Independence on July 4, 1776 and went to war with England. The Revolutionary War between America and England followed. The United States of America became its own country, just like Thomas Paine had said it should.

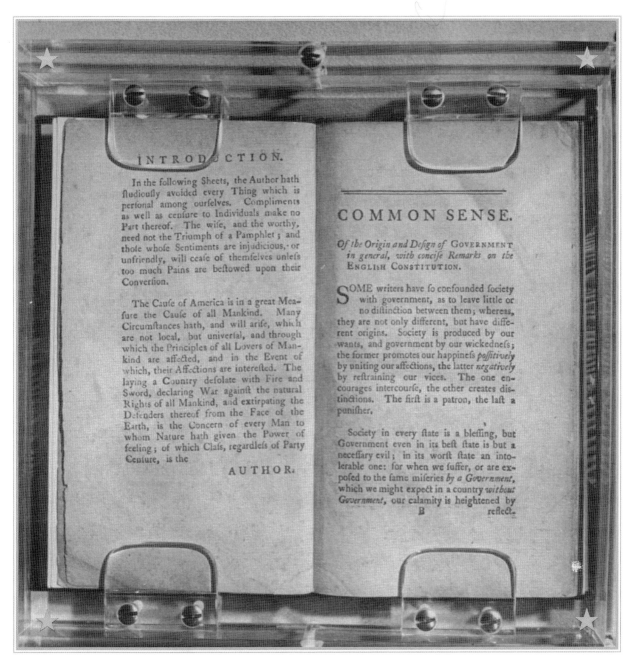

Thomas Paine's Common Sense *pamphlet*

A photograph of Paine's hometown of Thetford, England

Born in England

Thomas Paine was born on January 29, 1737. His parents lived in Thetford, England. This town is 70 miles (113 kilometers) northeast of the big city of London. Thetford was in the country, and it took two whole days to travel from there to the city. Back then, people traveled by walking, riding horses, or sitting in carriages pulled by horses.

The Paine family didn't have much money. Thomas's father made **corsets**, which women wore under their dresses in those days. It was hard work and didn't pay very well. Thomas wanted to do more with his life than make corsets like his father.

CORSETS

Many women of this era wore corsets under their dresses to make their waists look smaller and to add shape to their bodies. Corsets were made from cloth and pieces of bone from a whale. Making them was hard work.

Raised a Quaker

★

Most people in England belonged to the Church of England. The king of England was the head of this church. Members of this church are sometimes called "Anglicans." Thomas's father belonged to the Society of Friends, a group whose members are sometimes called **Quakers**.

Quakers didn't believe that there should ever be any wars. Thomas was raised in the Quaker faith, but he later decided that some wars were necessary. He thought America was right to go to war for its freedom.

QUAKERS

Quakers believed in worshiping in very simple fashion, without music or fancy churches. They were called Quakers after an early leader of the Society of Friends said they should "tremble (or 'quake') at the word of the Lord."

A typical gathering of Quakers

This statue in Thetford honors Thomas Paine.

School Days

When Thomas was a boy, it was hard to keep going to school if your parents didn't have much money. It cost money to go to school. And young boys like Thomas often needed to go to work to help the family make money.

Thomas did well in school. He really liked to read. But by the time he turned 13, he had to leave school to take a job. He went to work with his father, making corsets. It was boring work, and he hated it.

A horse and coach traveling in the English countryside

Off to Sea

★

By the time he was in his late teens, Thomas knew that he didn't want to spend his life making corsets. He wanted to see the world! In those days, lots of teenage boys took jobs working on ships and sailing at sea. Thomas ran away from home and took a job on a ship named the *King of Prussia*.

Working on the ship was hard. After three years, Thomas had had enough of it. When he returned to land, he took many different jobs. He collected taxes for the **government**, and he sold groceries and tobacco. He married twice, but his first wife died within the year, and he and his second wife separated after three years. He never had any children.

Young Paine sailed and worked on a ship like this one.

Benjamin Franklin persuaded Paine to go to America.

Meeting Benjamin Franklin

★

Thomas Paine's life changed after he met Benjamin Franklin in 1774. Franklin lived across the ocean in America, where England had 13 colonies. He came to London for a visit and met Thomas while he was there. Thomas had just written a paper on why tax collectors should be paid more, and Benjamin thought that Thomas was a very smart thinker and a good writer.

Benjamin told Thomas he should move to America. Since Thomas had recently separated from his second wife and had no good job, there was nothing to keep him in England. He sailed on a ship to America. In November, 1774, he found a new home in Philadelphia, Pennsylvania.

BENJAMIN FRANKLIN

One of the most famous men of the revolutionary period, Benjamin Franklin was a writer, a scientist, and an inventor. As a political leader, he helped gain support from France for America's battle for independence from England.

~

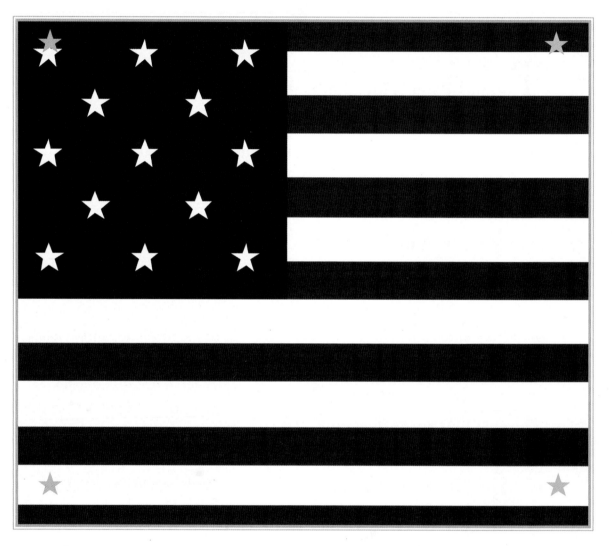

One of the flags that displayed 13 stars symbolizing the original 13 colonies

"Common Sense"

---★---

America was still ruled by England when Thomas moved there. Benjamin Franklin and other leaders felt that America should become its own country, and that the colonies should become the United States. Thomas agreed with them. In January of 1776, he published a pamphlet he had written titled *Common Sense*.

The pamphlet became very popular and sold many copies. Lots of people in America read Thomas's argument that the colonies should declare their independence from England. On July 4, 1776, America issued its Declaration of Independence, just as Thomas had said it should. What he called "common sense" inspired the American Revolution.

THE 13 COLONIES

Colonies are like states, only they belong to another country. When America declared its independence, it consisted of 13 colonies that were ruled by England. These colonies became the original United States.

~

A Fighter and a Writer

★

Thomas fought for what he believed in. Once the Revolutionary War started, he joined the army. He also continued to write a series of pamphlets titled *The Crisis* (or sometimes called *The American Crisis*).

In the first of these, he wrote his most famous line, "These are the times that try men's souls." (In this sentence, "try" means "challenge" or "bother.") General George Washington, the head of the American army, thought that Thomas's writing was so important that he had the pamphlet read out loud to his soldiers. He wanted them to know what they were fighting for and how important their battles were.

GEORGE WASHINGTON

George Washington was the general in charge of the American Revolutionary army. After America won the war, earned its freedom, and became a country, Washington was elected the first president of the United States.

~

George Washington thought Paine's writings were very important.

Paine donated money to help Americans fight against the English.

For the Love of His Country

★

The pamphlets by Thomas Paine became so popular that he was able to sell hundreds of thousands of them. Paine was still not a rich man because he refused to keep any of the money from selling the pamphlets. Instead, he gave all that money to help the cause of independence and to fight the war. He showed he was a great **patriot**, someone who truly loves his country.

Back to Europe

★

In 1787, Thomas Paine traveled back to Europe, visiting both England and France. He was not only a great writer, but he was also an **inventor.** He returned to England to try to raise money for a new type of bridge he had invented. This bridge was iron instead of wood or stone, and it didn't require posts in the middle of the river to hold it up.

Benjamin Franklin thought the bridge was a good idea, and he gave Thomas the names of people to visit in Europe who might help. Many bridges today have been built based on Paine's idea.

A portrait of Thomas Paine

Thomas Paine shown writing Rights of Man

"Rights of Man"

Thomas Paine strongly believed in freedom, for other countries as well as the United States. When a revolution started in France against that country's king, Thomas wrote a pamphlet that became very famous, titled *Rights of Man.* He published the first edition of this in 1791.

The booklet was banned in England, which also had a king. Thomas was considered a traitor. He thought that kings shouldn't rule people, but that people should rule themselves. This form of government is called **democracy**.

DEMOCRACY

Democracy is the form of government in which people vote to decide who will rule them and who will make the laws. America and France both had revolutions to get rid of government by a powerful king for a more democratic form of government.

~

"The Age of Reason"

★

In 1793, Paine got into trouble with the French government and was sent to prison. Even though he had been on the side of the French Revolution, he was against killing the king. He spent a year in jail.

While he was there, another of his great works, *The Age of Reason*, was published in 1794. The book was about religion and scientific reasoning. After his release from prison, Thomas Paine returned to America in 1802.

THE ENLIGHTENMENT

During the 1700s, a lot of great thinkers began using **reason** and science to explain things that were previously considered mysteries or matters of religious faith. This period was called "the **Enlightenment**," or "the Age of Reason."

~

Supporters of the French Revolution

A Great Patriot

★

When Thomas died in New York on June 8, 1809, he was known more for *The Age of Reason* than for earlier works such as *Common Sense*. John Adams became the second president of the United States. He said in 1806 that he didn't think "any man in the world has had more influence on its inhabitants or its affairs for the last thirty years than Thomas Paine."

Today, we remember Thomas Paine as a great patriot.

The home where Thomas Paine lived in New Rochelle, New York

Thomas Paine holding his Common Sense *pamphlet*

Time Line

1737 ★ Thomas Paine is born.

1750 ★ Thomas leaves school to start working for his father.

1750s ★ Thomas quits making corsets to sail the seas.

1774 ★ Thomas meets Benjamin Franklin and decides to sail to America.

1776 ★ Thomas publishes *Common Sense*, which influences the Declaration of Independence issued later that year.

1787 ★ Thomas sails back to Europe.

1793 ★ France sends Thomas to prison.

1794 ★ *The Age of Reason* is published before Thomas is released from prison.

1802 ★ Thomas returns to America.

1809 ★ Thomas dies in New York.

Glossary

corsets (KOR sutz) — old-fashioned forms of female underwear with hooks and laces

democracy (di MOK ruh see) — government by the people, who vote to elect their leaders

enlightenment (en LYT un munt) — seeing the light. A movement in the 1700s known as "The Enlightenment," or "The Age of Reason"

genius (JEE nyus) — a very smart person

government (GUV urn munt) — ruling body

independence (IN duh PEN dunts) — freedom from another government

inventor (in VENT ur) — someone who makes or discovers something brand new

pamphlet (PAM flut) — a small booklet or folded sheets of paper

patriot (PAY tree ut) — someone who loves his country very much and works hard for it

Quakers (KWAY KURZ) — members of a peace-loving religion known as the Society of Friends

reason (REEZ un) — using logic to figure something out and understand the world

Index

Further Reading

Blackbirch, Kate Davis. *Thomas Paine*. Gale Group, 2002.

McCarthy, Pat. *Thomas Paine: Revolutionary Patriot and Writer*. Enslow
    Publishers, Incorporated, 2001.

McCartin, Brian. *Thomas Paine: "Common Sense" and Revolutionary
    Pamphleteering*. The Rosen Publishing Group, 2002.

Websites to Visit

odur.let.rug.nl/~usa/B/tpaine/paine.htm

http://www.ushistory.org/paine/

http://libertyonline.hypermall.com/Paine/Default.htm

About the Author

Don McLeese is an award-winning journalist whose work has appeared in many newspapers and magazines. He earned his M.A. degree in English from the University of Chicago, taught feature writing at the University of Texas and has frequently contributed to the World Book Encyclopedia. He lives with his wife and two daughters in West Des Moines, Iowa.